U.S. PRESIDENTIAL ELECTIONS: HOW THEY WORK

PRESIDENTIAL NOMINATIONS

DANIELLE HAYNES

PowerKiDS press.

New York

Published in 2020 by The Rosen Publishing Group, Inc.
29 East 21st Street, New York, NY 10010

First Edition

Editor: Rachel Gintner
Book Design: Tanya Dellaccio

Photo Credits: Cover Bloomberg/Getty Images; p. 4 Jeff J Mitchell/Getty Images News/Getty Images; p. 5 Scott Olsen/Getty Images News/Getty Images; p. 7 (top) Jeff Greenberg/Universal Images Group/Getty Images; p. 7 (bottom) https://commons.wikimedia.org/wiki/File:Gilbert_Stuart_Williamstown_Portrait_of_George_Washington.jpg; p. 9 (both) Hulton Archive/Getty Images; p. 11 KENA BETANCUR/AFP/Getty Images; p. 12 David McNew/Getty Images News/Getty Images; p. 13 RJ Sangosti/Denver Post/Getty Images; p. 15 (top) Andrew Harrer/Bloomberg/Getty Images; p. 15 (bottom) JASON REDMOND/AFP/Getty Images; p. 17 ROBYN BECK/AFP/Getty Images; p. 19 (top) Steve Northup/The LIFE Images Collection/Getty Images; p. 19 (bottom) David Hume Kennerly/Archive Photos/Getty Images; p. 21 Ralph Morse/The LIFE Picture Collection/Getty Images; p. 23 Ralf-Finn Hestoft/Corbis News/Getty Images; pp. 24, 25 Bettmann/Getty Images; p. 27 Hill Street Studios/DigitalVision/Getty Images; p. 29 Hulton Archive/Archive Photos/Getty Images.

Cataloging-in-Publication Data

Names: Haynes, Danielle.
Title: Presidential nominations / Danielle Haynes.
Description: New York : PowerKids Press, 2020. | Series: U.S. presidential elections: how they work | Includes glossary and index.
Identifiers: ISBN 9781725310940 (pbk.) | ISBN 9781725310964 (library bound) | ISBN 9781725310957 (6 pack)
Subjects: LCSH: Presidents–United States–Nomination–Juvenile literature. | Presidents–United States–Election–History–Juvenile literature. | Presidential candidates–United States–History–Juvenile literature. | United States–Politics and government–Juvenile literature.
Classification: LCC JK521.H374 2020 | DDC 324.273'15–dc23

Manufactured in the United States of America

CPSIA Compliance Information: Batch #CWPK20. For Further Information contact Rosen Publishing, New York, New York at 1-800-237-9932.

CONTENTS

WHY WE NOMINATE

Every four years, Americans go to the polls to elect a new president. They do so by picking their favorite candidate on a list of names called a **ballot**. Usually, there are only a few presidential candidates on each state's ballot, one from each major party—Democratic and Republican—and sometimes independent or smaller party candidates.

PATH TO THE PRESIDENCY

PRESIDENTIAL ELECTIONS ARE SPLIT INTO TWO PARTS—FIRST, THE PRIMARY SEASON, THEN, THE GENERAL ELECTION. PRIMARY SEASON IS WHEN THE POLITICAL PARTIES HOLD PRIMARY ELECTIONS AND CAUCUSES TO DETERMINE WHICH CANDIDATES RECEIVE NOMINATIONS.

But imagine if everyone who wanted to run for president was listed on the ballot. There would be dozens—if not hundreds—of names, making it harder for voters to decide who to support and increasing the chances that no one candidate wins a majority of the vote.

This is one of the reasons why the United States uses a nomination process to narrow the field of candidates down to just a few people on Election Day.

ON THE BALLOT

In most states, there are very specific requirements a presidential candidate must fulfill in order to appear on the ballot in the general election. Candidates can do the following:

- The candidate can run as the nominee of a major political party recognized by the state.
- The candidate can run as an independent, which usually requires the individual get a certain number of **signatures** on a **petition** to qualify.
- Voters can write in a candidate of their choosing on the ballot, but only if the candidate registers with the state first.

Other than the first U.S. president, George Washington, every U.S. head of state has been the nominee of a major political party. This makes the nomination process a very important part of how we elect presidents.

Every four years, Americans vote for a new president, but the ballot includes several other races for Congress, local office, or state office. These are called downticket or downballot races.

GEORGE WASHINGTON

EARLY NOMINATIONS

In the nation's early days, members of Congress who belonged to the different parties decided which candidate to nominate for president. Some people disagreed with this process, because the Constitution says the legislative branch (Congress) and the executive branch (the president) must be separate. This problem was illustrated in 1812, when lawmakers in Congress said President James Madison had to declare war on Great Britain if he wanted to be nominated for a second term in office.

The **chaos** of the congressional nomination process in the 1824 election led to changes. That year, no candidate won the majority of votes, so the House of Representatives picked John Quincy Adams to be president—even though he had fewer votes than Andrew Jackson. The next election would be different, with the introduction of primaries!

PATH TO THE PRESIDENCY

THERE ARE THREE BRANCHES OF GOVERNMENT: THE EXECUTIVE (PRESIDENT), THE LEGISLATIVE (CONGRESS), AND JUDICIAL (THE COURTS). THE U.S. CONSTITUTION SAYS THESE BRANCHES MUST BE KEPT SEPARATE TO MAKE SURE NO ONE GROUP HAS TOO MUCH POWER.

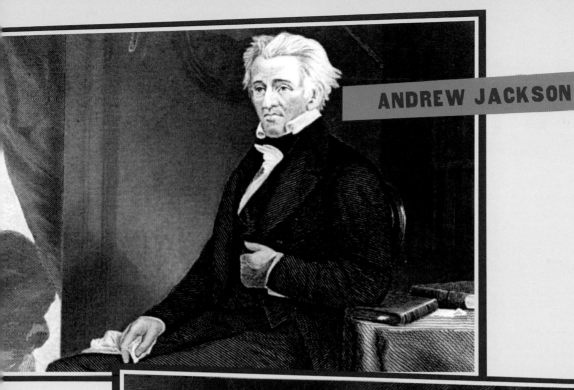

ANDREW JACKSON

JOHN QUINCY ADAMS

Even though Andrew Jackson won the most votes in the 1824 election, because there was no majority, the House of Representatives picked John Quincy Adams to be president.

9

BIG ANNOUNCEMENT

In current times, the nomination process is very different, because Congress is less involved and the American voters have a bigger role.

The first step in the process is that an individual has to announce their candidacy. They make a big announcement on TV or online, and they register with the political party that fits most closely with their views. Politicians who don't want be a part of a party can run as independents.

Candidates usually announce plans to run for president about a year and a half before Election Day. This gives them time to raise money for their campaign and tell voters what they stand for.

After announcing their run for the presidency, candidates start campaigning and traveling all over the country to get as much support as possible.

Donald Trump, who became the 45th president, announced his candidacy in a speech at Trump Tower alongside his family.

PATH TO THE PRESIDENCY

IN ORDER TO RUN FOR PRESIDENT, A CANDIDATE MUST BE A NATURAL-BORN CITIZEN OF THE UNITED STATES, MUST BE AT LEAST 35 YEARS OLD, AND MUST HAVE BEEN A RESIDENT OF THE UNITED STATES FOR AT LEAST 14 YEARS.

TRUMP
www.DonaldJTrump.com
MAKE AMERICA GREAT AGAIN!

HOW MANY CANDIDATES?

There's no limit to the number of people who can run for the presidential nomination of a political party. By spring 2019, more than 20 Democrats had announced their campaigns to seek their party's nomination! Many will drop out as they run out of money to campaign or fail to gather enough support to win the nomination.

2020 DEMOCRATIC CANDIDATE KAMALA HARRIS

A dozen Republicans ran for president in the 2016 election, though many dropped out throughout the primary season as they lost support and ran out of money.

When a president is running for reelection, there usually aren't many people in their own party who run against them for the nomination. It's assumed their political party will support the **incumbent** president for a second term in office.

The only elected president who failed to win their party's nomination for reelection was Franklin Pierce in the 1856 election. He lost the Democratic nomination to James Buchanan due to the way he handled certain issues.

PRIMARY SEASON

Between February and June of every election year, each state's political parties will either hold a primary or a caucus to determine which candidates receive nominations. Each party holds its own primary or caucus in each state. This means Republicans only compete against fellow Republican candidates and Democrats only compete against Democrats. Nominees from each party will run against each other in the general election.

In a primary, voters go to their local polling stations to pick which candidate they prefer in the political party of their choice. Caucuses are more **complicated**. In this process, select party members meet to discuss the candidates and pick who they think should be the nominee. Primaries are the most popular method and, in 2020, only six states will hold caucuses.

In some caucuses, like in Nevada, party members simply move to one side of a room to show their support for one candidate over another.

CAUCUS DAY AGENDA
SATURDAY • 2.20.2016

1. Registration
2. Temporary Precinct Chair calls caucus to order
3. Temporary Chair reviews caucus agenda
4. Reading of Letters
5. Contribution envelope passed
6. Election of Permanent Chair and Permanent Secretary
7. Announcement of viability threshold for the caucus
8. Presidential preference alignment(s)
9. Election of Delegates and Alternates
10. Submission of results to NV Dems HQ
11. Submission of nominations to County Central Committee
12. Submission of proposed county platform resolutions
13. New business
14. Caucus adjournment

HOW DOES A CAUCUS WORK?

CAUCUSES WERE ONCE THE MOST POPULAR METHOD OF PICKING A PARTY'S NOMINEE, BUT THE NUMBER OF STATES HOLDING THEM HAS DECLINED. NOT AS MANY VOTERS PARTICIPATE IN CAUCUSES BECAUSE THEY TAKE LONGER AND ARE HELD AT FEWER LOCATIONS COMPARED TO PRIMARIES. INSTEAD OF CASTING VOTES LIKE IN A PRIMARY, CAUCUS-GOERS GROUP TOGETHER BASED ON WHO THEY SUPPORT AND THEN DEBATE AND TRY TO PERSUADE UNCONVINCED VOTERS TO SUPPORT THEIR CANDIDATE. PARTICIPANTS CAN EVEN SWITCH SIDES!

THE ROLE OF DELEGATES

The outcomes of the primaries and caucuses determine how many delegates, or representatives from each state, will vote for a candidate when the primary season ends at each party's **convention**. The candidate who gets the most delegates at the convention usually receives the party's nomination.

Some states give all their delegates to the candidate who wins their primaries or caucuses. Others split up their delegates, giving more to candidates who got a greater share of votes. Each state has a certain number of delegates they can give a candidate depending on its population.

The Democratic Party also has superdelegates, who are representatives who cast a vote for whichever nominee they want, but only if the regular delegates are unable to decide upon a nominee.

PATH TO THE PRESIDENCY

Delegates attend their party's convention the summer before the general election and cast their votes to help select the party's presidential nominee. Delegates are active members of their political party in their home state.

THE CONVENTION

Both major political parties hold conventions the summer before the general election with the goal of nominating a candidate. The events usually last a few days.

The convention is a chance for political leaders to give speeches about the party's opinions on issues such as **immigration**, healthcare, the economy, and foreign policy. The parties also carry out official business, such as voting on new rules and appointing new leaders.

Delegates attend the conventions—held in different cities every four years—and cast their votes based on the results of their state's primaries and caucuses. The candidate who receives the majority of delegate votes wins the nomination. Americans usually know who will be nominated before the convention by counting the expected delegate votes after the primaries and caucuses.

The Republican Party selected former actor Ronald Reagan as its presidential candidate at the 1980 Republican National Convention in Detroit. He went on to be elected president twice.

...THER... A NEW BEGINNING

MICHIGAN

REPUBLICAN NATIONAL CONVENTION '80

REAGAN BUSH

REPUBLICAN NATIONAL CONVENTION, 2016

BROKERED CONVENTIONS

Though it's usually obvious who will receive a party's nomination at modern conventions, it is possible for no one candidate to receive a majority of delegates. If no candidate receives a majority in the first round of voting at the convention, it becomes a **brokered** convention.

When that happens, some or all delegates are released from rules requiring them to vote based on their states' primary and caucus results. They are allowed to vote for whomever they want in the second vote. At the Democratic National Convention, superdelegates are now allowed to join in the voting, too.

Brokered conventions were more common before states started using primary elections. Democrats also were more likely to have contested conventions before 1936, when they required two-thirds of the delegates to agree on a nominee.

The most recent brokered convention was in 1952 when Adlai Stevenson received the Democratic nomination.

CONVENTION SHENANIGANS

Conventions are festive events, with thousands of people in attendance wearing patriotic hats and pins. Some even wear an item of clothing to match fellow delegates from their home state—Texans may wear cowboy hats, and Hawaiians may wear flowered leis around their necks. Some attendees bring homemade signs showing support for their preferred candidate.

In addition to politicians, celebrities—such as Scarlett Johansson and Clint Eastwood—make speeches to help draw attention to their parties. In 2012, the Foo Fighters and Mary J. Blige performed at the Democratic National Convention, and Taylor Hicks and 3 Doors Down played at the Republican National Convention.

But things can turn chaotic, too. In 1924, while debating whether to **denounce** the racist Ku Klux Klan, Democrats broke out into a fistfight!

Rock band the Foo Fighters played at the 2012 Democratic National Convention in Charlotte, North Carolina, when President Barack Obama received the nomination for reelection.

THE NOMINEE SPEAKS

The final event on the final evening of the two major national conventions is reserved for the new presidential nominees to give an acceptance speech. The nominee uses this chance to not only lay out what issues are important to them, but also to generate support from the party as they head into the general election contest.

One reason why Franklin D. Roosevelt gave his acceptance speech in person was to prove he was still strong enough to lead the country, even though he was **paralyzed** from polio.

PICKING A VICE PRESIDENT

PRESIDENTIAL NOMINEES USUALLY ANNOUNCE THEIR RUNNING MATES—
OR VICE PRESIDENTIAL CANDIDATES—AT THE CONVENTIONS. THIS PERSON
HELPS THE CANDIDATE CAMPAIGN AND RAISE MONEY. BEFORE 1804,
THOUGH, THE PRESIDENTIAL CANDIDATE WHO CAME IN SECOND PLACE
IN THE ELECTION **AUTOMATICALLY** BECAME VICE PRESIDENT. THAT CAUSED
PROBLEMS WHEN THE FIRST- AND SECOND-PLACE CANDIDATES WERE FROM
DIFFERENT PARTIES AND DISAGREED ON POLITICS. IN 1796, JOHN ADAMS,
A MEMBER OF THE FEDERALIST PARTY, BECAME PRESIDENT AND THOMAS
JEFFERSON, A DEMOCRATIC-REPUBLICAN, BECAME VICE PRESIDENT.

In 2016, both Republican nominee Donald Trump and
Democratic nominee Hillary Clinton focused on bringing
groups of people together after a combative primary season.

President Franklin D. Roosevelt was the first presidential
nominee to deliver his acceptance speech in person at
the 1932 Democratic National Convention in Chicago. It
was during this speech that Roosevelt first mentioned the
economic program he came to be known for—the New Deal.

25

THE MAJOR PARTIES

There are multiple political parties in the United States, but for the most part, the country uses a two-party system. Since the 1860s, all U.S. presidents have been either Democrats or Republicans.

Other parties also hold conventions to nominate candidates for president. In 2016, the Green Party nominated Jill Stein and the Libertarian Party nominated Gary Johnson. The most recent successful **third-party** nominee was George Wallace, who won the support of several southern states in the 1968 election, when he ran as the American Independent Party candidate. He didn't become president.

Independent candidates run without a party nomination because they don't belong to a party. They must petition to be on each state's ballot, usually by collecting a certain number of signatures based on the population of the state.

IS A TWO-PARTY SYSTEM BEST?

THOUGH A TWO-PARTY SYSTEM CAN SIMPLIFY ELECTIONS BY GIVING VOTERS THE OPTION OF PICKING BETWEEN JUST TWO CANDIDATES, SOME PEOPLE DON'T LIKE HOW LIMITING IT CAN BE. WITH THE CURRENT SYSTEM, THIRD-PARTY CANDIDATES HAVE LITTLE CHANCE OF WINNING ELECTIONS, SO SOME VOTERS FEEL THAT A VOTE FOR THEM IS A WASTE OF A VOTE. AMERICANS WHO DON'T AGREE WITH THE TWO MAIN PARTIES CAN FEEL LIKE THEIR VIEWS AREN'T REPRESENTED IN GOVERNMENT AND MIGHT FEEL DISCOURAGED TO VOTE.

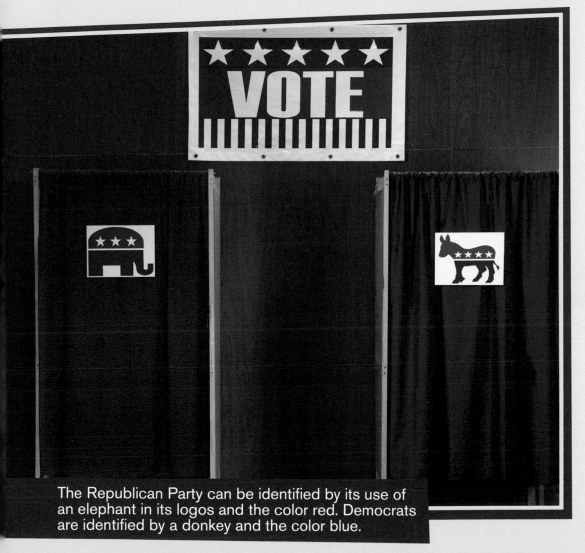

The Republican Party can be identified by its use of an elephant in its logos and the color red. Democrats are identified by a donkey and the color blue.

GENERAL ELECTION

Now that the parties have their nominees, they can put their support behind a single person to become president. This support often comes in the form of fundraising to help pay for the nominee's campaign.

During the months between the national conventions and Election Day, on the first Tuesday after November 1, the nominees campaign and debate against each other.

Their goal is to get enough votes in each state to earn all the electors from the state. Instead of a **popular vote**, presidents are elected using the Electoral College method, in which each state has a certain number of electors to give to the candidate who wins the most votes. There are 538 total electors, and the candidate who gets at least 270 wins the presidency.

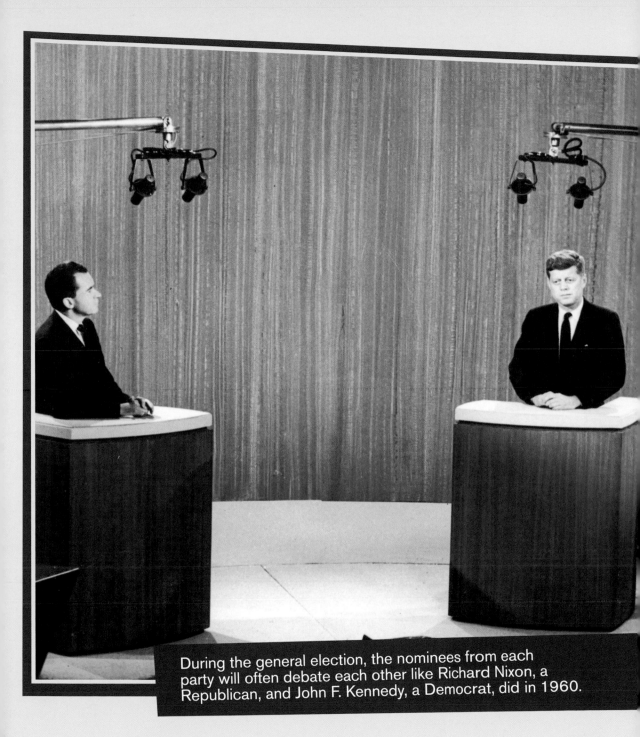

During the general election, the nominees from each party will often debate each other like Richard Nixon, a Republican, and John F. Kennedy, a Democrat, did in 1960.

MAKE YOUR VOICE HEARD

Election season can be a long process, with dozens of candidates holding countless rallies to get as many votes as possible. But imagine if the major parties didn't nominate someone. Up to a dozen candidates from each party could run the race for a year and a half all the way until Election Day!

It's likely no one would earn the 270 electors necessary to win, because too many candidates would share the vote. If that happened, the House of Representatives, one of the two bodies in Congress, would elect the president from the three candidates who received the most votes.

So nominations—and the primaries and caucuses used to determine the nominee—are a key way for Americans to make sure their voices are heard under the current U.S. election system.

GLOSSARY

automatically: Happening or done without deliberate thought or effort.

ballot: A sheet of paper or digital screen voters use to pick candidates.

brokered: Something that is arranged through discussion.

chaos: A state of confusion.

complicate: To make difficult.

convention: A large meeting of people at a central location.

denounce: To declare that you disagree with someone.

immigration: The act of traveling from one country to another to seek permanent residence.

incumbent: The person who already holds a political office and wants to be reelected.

paralyzed: Unable to move part or all of your body.

petition: A document with signatures making a request.

popular vote: Electing someone to public office by counting all individual voters, not electors.

signature: Signing your name to something.

third-party: A person who runs for office under a party other than Democratic or Republican.

INDEX

WEBSITES

Due to the changing nature of Internet links, PowerKids Press has developed an online list of websites related to the subject of this book. This site is updated regularly. Please use this link to access the list: www.powerkidslinks.com/uspe/nominations